100

Things to Do In & Around Historic

St. Charles

Ann Hazelwood

Cover design by Benjamin Pierce.
Inside layout design by Eric Winters.
Edited by Fran Levy.
Photographs by Ann Hazelwood, Marian Brickner and courtesy of the Christmas Tradition Committee and the Greater St. Charles Convention and Visitors Bureau.

Printed in the United States of America

ISBN 1-891442-39-2
Library of Congress: Pending

Virginia Publishing Company
625 N. Euclid, Suite 330
P.O. Box 4538
St. Louis, MO 63108
www.STL-Books.com

Dedication

This handbook is dedicated to the Citizens of St. Charles, Missouri, who continue to amaze me with their creativity and their willingness to make the quality of life in St. Charles the very best that it can be. I am very proud to be a citizen of this great community!

I have been blessed with their business, friendship and talent.

THANK YOU, ST. CHARLES!

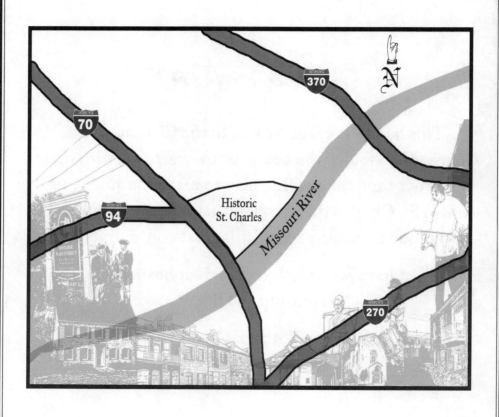

Historic
St. Charles

Missouri River

Introduction

As the operator of a business for more than 25 years in a tourist area, I am asked on a daily basis about other activities in the community. Naturally, I am attached to the Historic area of St. Charles because it is the area I know best and love the most. Pride in my community takes me places that are worth telling you about in this great city.

When I mention businesses, I am giving you an unsolicited list of things to experience that I love or that I know are popular in our community. If the events are repeated in a timely fashion each year, they may lead you to create your own personal traditions.

I extend a special thank you to our Greater St. Charles Visitors and Convention Bureau, which continually advertises all the great places and events. I hope that in writing this guide I have encouraged you to try some of these wonderful experiences. I also hope that I succeed in encouraging you to create your own.

ANN HAZELWOOD

MARIAN BRICKNER PHOTO

BOAT HOUSE AND NATURE CENTER

~ 1 ~

Boat House and Nature Center

Located right on the Missouri River is the awesome Lewis and Clark museum, which is open every day. St. Charles was the send-off location of Lewis and Clark's historic trip in 1804. You'll experience special exhibits, watch a video about Lewis and Clark's trail, and see a magnificent view of the river. Built in 2004, the museum also houses the replica keel boats used to reenact the famous trip. This is a MUST if you visit St. Charles.

~ 2 ~

Lunch in the Park

If you love the beautiful riverfront that St. Charles has to offer, you'll enjoy the pastoral Frontier Park even better with a lunch on one of the park's picnic tables. Delis from nearby Main Street will be happy to pack you a basket.

BON APPETIT.

~ 3 ~

Renew Your Vows

No matter what your religion or where you were married, you might consider a romantic outdoor wedding in the Main Street Gazebo, in the 400 block of South Main Street, to renew your wedding vows. Most Saturdays, this charming gazebo is busy with weddings or wedding photos. Many arrive in a horse-drawn carriage to this historic setting. Call the St. Charles Parks Department to make reservations for a group.

~ 4 ~

Ride the Trolley

Enjoy seeing our historic districts at a much slower pace by riding the St. Charles Trolley. Ask informed drivers about places of interest. There are trolley stops so that you can get on and off at your leisure.

~ 5 ~

Take a Carriage Ride

There's nothing more romantic than a horse-drawn carriage to escort you around the historic district of St. Charles. Whether you prefer a silent horseman — perhaps so that you can have privacy for a wedding proposal — or a verbal guided tour, the carriage will accommodate your needs. You'll always remember the sounds of the clip-clopping on the brick streets of St. Charles.

QUILTS ON MAIN

~ 6 ~

Quilts on Main

Hundreds of quilts hanging on 14 blocks of buildings create an artistic setting you will never forget. Originated in 2001, this nationally known attraction continues to grow every year. It is held annually on the second Saturday of September from 9:00 a.m. to 5:00 p.m. You'll not only see the quilts, but special exhibits and guests are always scheduled. Additional days of quilt-related activities are also planned by the organizers from Main Street First, a business organization on South Main. For year 'round information, go to www.quiltsonmain.com

~ 7 ~

Home Town Pizza

Everyone in St. Charles knows the Italian Restaurant called "Pio's," in downtown St. Charles at 4th and First Capitol Streets. Three generations have been serving the "best pizza in town" at this location. It's my favorite pizza, with a very thin crust and a secret combination of cheeses. For those who move away, it's a must to visit "Pio's" when they return. Eat your heart out, New York.

~ 8 ~

A Moonlight Stroll

We are so fortunate that the Missouri Riverfront borders the eastern edge of the city of St. Charles. Many activities are held in the riverfront park because of its beauty. Many love to watch the sunrise or the sunset in this tree-lined background. It's a nice, one-mile walk on the park pathway, or you can choose the hiking trail that aligns itself to the park. I recommend taking time out to sit on one of the convenient benches and just soak up nature.

~ 9 ~

It's Frontier Fridays in the Summer

If you're in St. Charles on a Friday night June through September, you'll "party in the park," which is our Frontier Park on the riverfront. From 5:00 p.m to 10:00 p.m., a new band will perform on the Jaycee stage. The St. Charles Jaycees will be happy to serve you refreshments, with proceeds benefiting their many worthwhile causes in the community.

~ 10 ~

Back Door Sale

You're welcome in the front door of the South Main shops, but it's at the back door where you'll get the very best, rock bottom, garage sale prices. Because of outdoor restrictions in the historic area, we keep our "trashy treasures" to a twice-a-year sale on one day each in spring and fall, from 8:00 a.m. to 12:00 p.m. Check with any shop owner for the date of the next bargain bash.

~ 11 ~

Trick or Treat

The evening before Halloween, everyone comes to Historic Main Street to see thousands of people dressed for the Halloween Trick or Treat event, sponsored by the South Main Preservation Society. It was started many years ago to give back to the community. You will see unbelievable costumes worn by grownups as well as children, parading shoulder to shoulder to collect the generous handouts from Main Street merchants. You know it's Halloween when you experience this hometown event.

~ 12 ~

Our History of Flowers

Parkview Gardens has showered the city of St. Charles with flowers since 1929. Located near historic Blanchette Park on Randolph Street, they add such beauty as you enter this sizeable floral nursery owned by the Gillette family. In downtown St. Charles, across from our St. Joseph Hospital, is Buse's Flower Shop, which has been doing business for 40 years. Their floral creations are never a disappointment. The two families have become institutions in our community, and their dedication and generosity amazes us. Call Parkview at 636-946-1925 and Buse's at 636-724-0148.

~ 13 ~

Lenten Fish Fries

Even though you may not be a practicing church member, you will know it's the beginning of Lent by the smell of the fish frying around town. Many Catholic Churches raise funds by having fish dinners on Friday night. St. Peter's Church on First Capitol Drive in downtown St. Charles is one of the more popular places to be seen indulging in outdoor fish frying. The large sign and bustle of activity near the street will make the church easy for you to find. Inside the church hall, you'll be able to purchase a "take home" dinner or partake of all the trimmings of a church supper, including cold beer.

~ 14 ~

Festival of the Little Hills
(Les Petite Cotes)

We celebrate our heritage BIG time in St. Charles with an annual craft and food festival on the third full weekend of August. Started in 1975 to be a quality event of authentic crafts, the festival grew into an enormous three-day event with free entertainment and booths representing many nonprofit organizations. Main Street is closed to traffic to accommodate visitors from all over the country. You must experience the event everyone looks forward to, because it puts money in the community's treasury and offers a social opportunity for all of us -- and I hope, for YOU as well.

THE FAMOUS COCONUT CREAM PIE

~ 15 ~

Best Pie in Town

Every hometown has a place to get the best piece of pie in town. For more than 20 years, the Mother-In-Law House, located in the 500 block of historic South Main, has been serving its specialty, coconut cream pie, which will delight you with its beauty and taste. Owner Donna Hafer has the secret to a flaky crust and mellow coconut filling. When I want to impress someone for lunch or dinner, I entertain them in this Victorian atmosphere, where I know they will get the best of Donna's attention and the best pie in town.

~ 16 ~

Concert in the Park

Every community should have the experience we have in St. Charles with our Municipal Band. Established more than 100 years ago, it continues to present outdoor concerts every Thursday evening at 8:00 p.m., starting in June and running through September. Bring your own lawn chair or blanket if you prefer, and refresh yourself with your own beverages or those provided for purchase. Every age group enjoys the variety of music and riverfront park atmosphere.

~ 17 ~

Unique Dining Experience

One of the most unique and first-class dining experiences
I have ever had in St. Charles was at a private dining
establishment called the Hamilton House, located at 325 S.
Main, in the Historic area. Call 636-949-8899 to find out
when their next theme dinner is planned. Hamilton House is
owned and operated by two young, married chefs, trained in
France, who are creating a fine dining experience in their own
historic home — they reside upstairs. They can also arrange
a special group dinner. I have experienced one, and people are
still talking about it.

~ 18 ~

Take a Walking Tour of the Commons Historic Neighborhood

St. Charles is blessed with many historic neighborhoods. What is known as "The Commons" was once common ground outside the Village of St. Charles where animals and crops were shared. As the village grew, the common area began to develop with small, charming houses, schools and churches. As you walk this neighborhood adjacent to the Frenchtown area, you'll notice that attractive signs are placed in each yard, telling you the date and the name of the family that built the house. Every other year, the neighborhood holds a house tour.

~ 19 ~

Actions and Thrills

It is not only the kids with you who will enjoy the Demolition Ball, located on 1860 Sheer Parkway. The slogan is, "where fun and action come alive." There are two courts for the bumper cars, as well as amusements such as video games to please you. If that's too much action, the movie theater next door will entertain the party poopers. Check it out at www.demolitionball.com

~ 20 ~

Photo at Area Landmark

On the campus of Lindenwood University is the famous, historic crooked tree. This leaning, live, beautiful tree is located on the corner of the busy intersection of Kingshighway and First Capitol Drive. Despite the area's development, this tree his been protected by the community's admiration for its unique shape. This is a perfect photo backdrop that will help you identify your visit to St. Charles and Lindenwood University. SMILE.

~ **21** ~

Christmas Traditions

From Thanksgiving to Christmas, you will want to hang out as much as you can on Historic Main Street. You'll enjoy the decorations, made with live greenery and hundreds of red velvet bows, as well as the sound of the St. Charles Fife and Drum Corps and the groups of carolers all along the street. Authentically dressed Santas representing many different countries will hand out collector's cards to all the children. Across from my shop in the 300 block is the dapper gentleman roasting chestnuts on an open fire -- it doesn't get any better. More attractions are added to this longtime tradition each year, and you won't want to miss any of them.

100 Things to Do In & Around Historic *St. Charles*

CHRISTMAS TRADITION COMMITTEE

CAROLING THROUGH ST. CHARLES

~ 22 ~

Carol with Us

Los Posadas is one of the biggest caroling events in the country. This mile-long parade of warmly dressed carolers follow "Joseph and Mary" riding on a donkey. This longtime tradition brings in visitors from outlying states. Many carry lanterns as they stroll down the historic street. "Mary and Joseph" stop at several locations to see if there is any room at the inn. The caroling ends at the Frontier Park's band stage, where additional entertainment is offered. The Mayor then lights the large tree nearby. You can then warm up by the bonfire and enjoy some refreshments.

~ 23 ~

Go Back in Time at the "Hangar's Dance"

One of the huge hangars at St. Charles Municipal Airport is the nostalgic site for the Annual Hangar's Dance. To the sounds of a big band, hundreds dress in WWII attire to relive the days of war and romance. There is an award for the best-dressed attendee, who might be wearing the uniform of an armed service or even a nurse of the era. The dance takes place the beginning of October. Call 636-946-6066 for directions.

~ 24 ~

The Festival of Ice

FÊTE DE GLACE is an outdoor show of ice sculptures, presented in the dead of winter. As you stroll up and down Historic North Main, you'll see sculptors carving their artistic creations as they compete for prizes. It is fascinating to see the shapes appear before your eyes. Don't worry about the cold; there are outdoor warm-up fireplaces and hot refreshments to make this a must-see event in late January.

~ 25 ~

A Tour of Great Importance

The Academy of the Sacred Heart/Shrine of St. Philippine Duchesne is located in the heart of the French settlement in our city. It is the site of the first free school west of the Mississippi. It was established in 1818 by Mother Rose Philippine Duchesne, canonized in 1988. The shrine is open daily from 9:00 a.m. to 4:00 p.m., but if you desire a tour, which I recommend, call ahead.

The phone number is 636-946-5632.

~ 26 ~

A Little Gambling Fun?

Ameristar Casino, located on the Missouri Riverfront, has the largest selection of gaming in the region. Poker is quite the hot pasttime now; however there are many venues to challenge your luck. I have enjoyed great food at their seven dining areas. St. Charles has benefited greatly from the casino's success. It's a city all its own.

ART IN THE MAKING AT THE FOUNDRY

~ 27 ~

View Art at the Foundry

You won't believe what has been done to this historic Car Foundry. Once an active factory, this huge facility has been redesigned for local artists to create their work in studios on the second-floor balcony. On the entry level are galleries and a gift shop. Educational opportunities are available, as well as regularly scheduled performing arts. The class and culture this facility provides are priceless. To see what's happening now, go to www.foundryartcentre.org

~ 28 ~

Visit St. Charles' Oldest Grocery Store

Privately owned for more than 20 years, the Mid-Towne IGA store, at 317 Hawthorne Shopping Plaza, is where all the locals not only get their weekly groceries but the latest news from their friends and neighbors. Early in the morning, you'll see a line for the fresh bakery goods, like their hot glazed donuts. Around dinner hour, working people are lined up to take home a delicious meal from the hot deli. The store opens early and closes late. Their number is 636-724-7500.

~ 29 ~

A Tea Room Experience

If this sounds good to you, there's no question that Miss Amy B's is the place to visit for a rich taste of history and incredible food. Located in a beautiful, 1865 mansion at 837 First Capitol Drive, it is a charming tea room with boutique shops on the second floor. I have many favorites in the Tea Room, but the French toast is to die for, and you get lots of personal attention at breakfast and lunch. Reservations are not taken, but there is much to see and enjoy while you wait.

~ 30 ~

Frozen Custard, Anyone?

If you ask any "local" where they go on a hot summer's night for a nice hot fudge sundae or the best ice cream cone in town, they will tell you about Lyon's Custard, at 2309 Elm Street. After you choose your delight, you'll want to visit with many who congregate in the gazebo nearby. You may see your next door neighbor or a visitor from Arkansas. My favorite memory is the time when I accidentally dropped my custard cone into my purse when I paid. I hope that will only be MY memory.

~ 31 ~

Wine by a Fire

No matter what the season, a glass of wine in the romantic setting of the Little Hills Winery will impress your business associate, lover or friend. Beautiful landscaping lines the sidewalk at 501 S. Main. You can watch the walkers go by or gaze at the other historic structures nearby. Outdoor fireplaces comfort you on chilly nights in the garden of this historic wine establishment. Here's to you!

~ 32 ~

Bluegrass Festival

Missouri is gifted with many musicians, and you'll hear quite a few fiddle their favorite tunes and stomp their feet on the second Saturday in September, in partnership with the Civil War Days event. Bring your blanket or lawn chair, because you'll want to stay and enjoy all the activity on our riverfront. Yee haw!

~ 33 ~

Art on the Street

On North Main, the third weekend of September, you'll be very pleased to see fantastic art in various media displayed and marketed in white tents. The Mosaics Festival of the Arts attracts artists across from around the country for your enjoyment and the opportunity to purchase. It's a great opportunity to buy unique gifts to stash away for Christmas, which I do every year. The children's area and food booths will enhance your visit.

CIVIL WAR REENACTMENT

~ 34 ~

Civil War Reenactment

The history of the 1860s certainly comes alive on the second Saturday and Sunday of September. Approximately 400 reenactors recreate battles, including period costumes and even the animals of that period in time. Listen to the cannons shoot and learn more about the Civil War.

~ 35 ~

See the China

Wait until you see what the Haviland Museum has to offer
St. Charles. In a historic home on the National Register
at 625 S. Main, you'll be able to have a guided tour of the
most diversified Haviland china that you will ever see. Local
businesswoman Donna Hafer collected these marvelous sets
throughout her lifetime. Call for an appointment 636-925-
0745 for one of my favorite places to see.

~ 36 ~

Fireworks on the Hill

If you are going to be in St. Charles for July 4th, you'll enjoy one of the choicest spots for viewing a spectacular fireworks display on the hill of the St. Charles County Court House. It's tradition to bring your blanket or chairs to sit on this landscaped county landmark and enjoy not only the sparklers, but the awesome view of the Missouri River.

Some years, there are two evening opportunities to celebrate the Riverfest fireworks display.

~ 37 ~

Rent a Bike

If you are caught in St. Charles without a bike, do not fear. Help is handily located at the Touring Cyclist, at 104 N. Main. Bike rental is a big activity in this full-service bicycle shop, which backs up to the famous Katy Trail. Many brands are there for you to sample and even purchase. Main Street and local trails are perfect for this venue. The folks at the shop will be happy to assist you with your route plan and tell you about cool things to look for along your way.

~ 38 ~

Music on Main

This is one of the happiest events you will experience. If you love music, fun, laughter, networking and spirits, you'll love Music on Main, sponsored by the North Main Business organization. On the first Wednesday of each month, May through September, at 5:30 p.m., you'll enjoy a different style of music and great entertainment. You'll see business attire on the working folks, casual jeans and leisure outfits on the young and retired. A good hot dog might top off a fun evening. If you want to sit and listen, bring a lawn chair; or, if you care to dance, the street is blocked off for your enjoyment.

MARIAN BRICKNER PHOTO

TRAILHEAD BREWING COMPANY

~ 39 ~

Sample Brew

Yes, we make our own brew. It's "heads up" when you experience the wonderful brews at the Trailhead Brewing Company at Main and Boones Lick, in the historic area. This interesting building was an old grist mill, but now it contains handcrafted beers brewed right on the premises. There are three floors of interesting décor, and the restaurant offers great food to complement your beverage. My favorite is the BBQ chicken pizza. This is one of the more fun, casual dining or luncheon experiences.

~ 40 ~

A Tintype Photo

There's an experience waiting for you at the Tintype Photo Parlor that will take you back in time and capture you in a photograph for a keepsake. It's fun to try on the different period styles of clothing while deciding who you want to portray. Hand tinting is available, as are many wonderful frames from which to choose. The shop is located at 510 S. Main in the historic area and is open daily. See samples for yourself on their Web site, www.tintypephotoparlour.com. Smile.

~ 41 ~

Chocolate and Cookies

Who wouldn't want to experience 30 homemade varieties of cookies that are baked daily at J. Noto's Fine Confectionery? How about 75 varieties of chocolate and delicious desserts, not to mention flavored coffees? Located across from my shop at 336 S. Main, this tempting establishment lures in a steady stream of customers. You'll be impressed that it is operated by three generations of family, so please introduce yourself to these delightful folks. And leave your diet behind.

~ 42 ~

Sample Homemade Fudge

Every good city needs a fudge maker, and a fine one we have. Jim and Kathy Brown operate Riverside Sweets at 416 S. Main, and you'll likely find Jim standing there making more delicious fudge. You'll be able to indulge in other goodies, such as scooped ice cream and seasonal packaged treats, and sample the 45 flavors of Jelly Bellys. After you purchase your goodies, you'll want to sit on a bench near the gazebo next door and tease passersby with your wonderful treat.
Eat your heart out.

~ 43 ~

Create Your Own Jewelry

Imagine picking out just the right beads and stones that are your very favorites and putting them into a customized piece of jewelry. Janice Boschert has operated String Along With Me for a long time and has a flare for fashion that will help you create that very piece that you desire. Other accessories will tempt you there as well. Her location is on the lower level of the historic Newbill McKilhiny House, in the 600 block of South Main.

~ 44 ~

Stay at a First-Class RV Park

Not all of us have the luxury to travel in an RV, but if you have the opportunity, the "Sundermeier RV Park" at 111 Transit Street is for you! I am amazed at what this park has available for the 114 parking sites. It's open all year long and offers you the luxuries of home. Carolyn and Bill Strong will not only be your host, but also help you explore the community! This park along the Katy Trail has been ranked 12th in the U.S., and their nearby eating establishment, "Beefeaters Pub and Grill," was voted best restaurant by Motor Home Magazine. Call toll free, 1-800-929-0832, or visit www.sundermeierpark.com

~ 45 ~

Discover Our French Heritage

A recently restored Frenchtown Heritage Museum is
located at 1400 N. Second Street, right in the heart of
the Frenchtown settlement in St. Charles. This museum
is housed in an 1880s firehouse and contains not only an
outstanding collection of Frenchtown memorabilia, but
displays of old trains and firefighter artifacts. It is run by
volunteers and is open Wednesdays through Saturdays from
12:00 to 3:00 p.m. Call 636-946-8682 if you need a special
appointment. We are fortunate to have this museum to help
tell about the French history in St. Charles.

MISSOURI'S FIRST STATE CAPITOL

~ 46 ~

Visit Missouri's First State Capitol

Yes, it's here in St. Charles, not Jefferson City. This perfectly restored building is furnished as it appeared from 1821 to 1826. You will sense the historical presence of the time when you take a tour that is offered daily by the Missouri Department of Natural Resources. This must-see site is located in the heart of the historic area in the 200 block of South Main Street. During the holiday season, you could attend one of the candlelight music concerts. Check out your options on their Web site www.dnr.state.mo.us

~ 47 ~

Attend a Book Signing

Main Street Books, located at 621 S. Main, has regularly scheduled book signings by mostly local authors. This small, quaint shop is located in the Collier Cottage Schoolhouse and prides itself on carrying many unique books about St. Charles history. Great personal service from owner Mary Fran Rash has been one of the reasons for the shop's success. Upstairs you'll find a great children's library, popular with many young folks. Call 636-946-3736 to order any book or check the Web site at www.mainstreetbooks.net to see who might be signing.

~ 48 ~

Taste a Variety of Hot Wings from Many Restaurants

There is an annual "Wing Ding" on the grounds of the popular Bass Pro Shop. This always sold-out event is held the first part of June, with proceeds benefiting the Boone Center Workshop, a nonprofit organization that helps adults with disabilities. The hours are 4:30 to 8:00 p.m. It's only $20.00, and that entitles you to two drink tickets and all the chicken wings you can eat. Call 636-978-4300 or check it out on the Web at www.boonecenter.com.

MARIAN BRICKNER PHOTO

BIKING ON THE KATY TRAIL

~ 49 ~

Hike or Bike the Trail

A convenient place to get on the magnificent Katy Trail that runs across our county is to go to Frontier Park by the 16-acre riverfront. There are sheltered, printed maps that guide you to wherever you might like to venture on the trail. The scenic route is like none other. There are small towns and special views where you may want to stop and rest. Some take advantage of the many wineries and B&Bs along the way. We are fortunate in this community to have this trail at our fingertips.

~ 50 ~

Have a Family Reunion

It's a St. Charles tradition for many, many years to go to Blanchette Park and revisit your childhood memories in the same playground and pavilions that you previously enjoyed. If you are a new visitor, you'll be impressed with the new family aquatic pool, three tennis courts, 12 horseshoe courts and three athletic fields. On the 42 acres, you'll see activities all year long, including a busy snow sledding hill in the dead of winter. Blanchette Hall is a nicely restored facility that is used for many of the town's social functions, including classes and events from the Parks and Recreational Department.

~ 51 ~

Take a Guided Tour of Historic South Main

South Main is the largest designated Historic District in the state of Missouri. It features nearly 100 buildings that date from 1790 to the late 1800s. Many of these charming buildings are now specialty shops and dining establishments that make you want to visit again. You can pick up information for a self-guided tour or request a docent at the Greater St. Charles Convention and Visitors Bureau. Walking in the footsteps of early pioneers on the bricks and cobblestones will give you a sense of the past, as well as introduce you to the present.

LEARN TO QUILT

~ 52 ~

Learn to Quilt: You Can Do This

The Midwest is rich in its tradition of quilting, for men and women alike. It's a community where women still gather to quilt each week at the local churches and attend a Quilt Social most any weekend. For more than 100 years, Huning's Department Store on North Main kept the craft alive, until its demise in the 1980s. Patches etc., at 337 S. Main, opened in 1979 and continues to service quilters to this day, including its efforts to produce Quilts On Main. The popular slogan from Patches etc. can apply to you as well: "You Can Do This."

~ 53 ~

Walk the Boone's Lick Trail

Historians have told us about Daniel Boone coming down Boone's Lick Road in 1820. Out of it grew the Santa Fe Salt Lick and Oregon Trails. A five-block road from 5th Street to Main Street was restored in 2004 for visitors to use as an entrance to the Historic Area from the Interstate. Gaslights, sidewalks, benches and posted information on walking tours are placed along this trail, and there is a plank road bridge with an authentic wagon to show what the trail was originally like.

~ 54 ~

Celebrate the Scottish Heritage

On the first Saturday in April, you'll see plaids a-popping everywhere. Scottish clans from all over Missouri will gather on Main Street for one of the most outstanding parades that this city ever sees. The color and sounds of the bagpipes will certainly put you in the Scottish mood, and you'll follow the parade to Frontier Park, where competitive games are held. This event is called "Tartan Days" and should not be missed. Learn more at www.tartanfestivities.com.

~ 55 ~

View a Permanent Car Show

If you love classic cars and all the memorabilia that go with them, you are in for a treat when you visit Fast Lane Classic Cars at 427 Little Hills Boulevard in north St. Charles. This really cool showroom has 45,000 square feet of show space, including two indoor showrooms of beautifully restored cars and bikes of all kinds. The gift shop is certainly an attraction for everyone, whether or not you are a car enthusiast. This is a treat for the whole family.

~ 56 ~

Tour the St. Charles Convention Center

You won't believe that a Convention Center could be warm, attractive and artistic. You don't have to attend a convention to see the wonderful amenities that this first-class facility has to offer. The Grand Ballroom of 16,200 square feet features hand-painted murals of Lewis and Clark that you won't want to miss. The Cyber Space Café has complimentary Internet services as part its user-friendly atmosphere. Located right off Interstate 70, the Convention Center is easy to find. For more information, call toll free, 1-877-896-7227, or visit www.stcharlesconventioncenter.com.

HISTORIC NEIGHBORHOOD

~ 57 ~

Sleep Near an Old Elm Tree

The beautiful, Victorian, wraparound porch Bed and Breakfast is a place I am proud to recommend for a delightful night's sleep. I have stayed there, enjoying wine on a gorgeous patio under the oldest elm tree in St. Charles, and indulged in a three-course breakfast the next morning. Owner Martha Koojumjian is charming and a stickler for detail. I guarantee you that a stay at 1717 Elm Street will never be forgotten. Make reservations well in advance, because it is a popular place. The phone number is 636-947-4843.

~ 58 ~

Attend a Hockey Game

The Missouri River Otters are a fast and mighty professional hockey team of which we are quite proud. They play in the beautiful arena at 2002 Arena Parkway, just minutes from downtown. The season runs October through April, so you'll want to check for scheduling at www.riverotters.com. Don't forget a souvenir from their gift shop.

~ 59 ~

Take a Mini-Cruise

The ST. CHARLES EMPRESS offers daytime and twilight cruises that provide a tour of the coastline of the Missouri River. Directly behind the 500 block of South Main you will see this luxurious motor yacht waiting along the river for your personal enjoyment. Groups with special occasions could also benefit from this romantic and scenic experience. Call 636-946-4995 to make your reservation.

~ 60 ~

Dinner Cooked at Your Tableside

Shogun Japanese Steak and Sushi, at 2057 Zumbehl Road, will give you a show as well as some really good food. They really like to honor you on a special occasion, so keep that in mind. If you want a little shakeup in your normal dining experience, check this out. This is a grand place to invite others to join you. Call 636-940-2090 for more information.

~ 61 ~

Plan Your Own Progressive Dinner

Here are a few suggestions on how to sample more than one restaurant in an evening. Start with some crab cakes from Oliver's on Historic North Main Street. They are excellent, especially with the house Merlot. Then move to the Ameristar Casino's 47 Port Street Grill for a heavenly porterhouse steak. Order dessert at the Lewis and Clark Restaurant and Public House, at 217 S. Main. You'll want the Missouri Mud Pie, which combines two of my favorite things, chocolate and ice cream. It's time to take a walk down the street to Old Mill Stream Inn, at 912 S. Main, where you can relax with an after-dinner drink or one of their many choices of beer. You are likely to hear a guitar player. Relax by the creek and waterfall. Now it's up to YOU where you lay your head tonight.

~ 62 ~

Attend an Auction

There's a joke in our town that you could attend an auction on any day of the week, because they are so popular. If you are an antiquer, you'll love the estate and farm auctions listed in the local newspapers each week. They are held outdoors and indoors. If you want your money to go to charity, there is a nonprofit event almost any weekend, and sometimes two or three of them. Some very good buys are commonly made; and, if you paid too much, I'm certain the good time was well worth the money.

~ 63 ~

Find out about Your Family Name

Thistle and Clover, at 330 S. Main, can do that for you when you visit their heraldry department for the history of your family name and its coat of arms. Not only can they research it right there on the computer, but they will print it on document paper ready for framing. If you need a frame for it, they can supply that as well. While you're there, shop for delightful Irish and Scottish gifts to take home.

Call 636-946-2449 for more information.

~ 64 ~

Feast at a Church Supper

This community has a tremendous amount of German cooks. Most churches all over the county love church suppers, where you get home-cooked turkey, dressing, sausage, sauerkraut and green beans. If you have room, you'll love all the desserts, especially home-baked pies. In St. Charles, you need to check with Immanuel Lutheran Church at 6th and Jefferson, the First United Methodist Church on 801 First Capitol, and the Friedens United Church of Christ on Zumbehl and Hwy. 94. These are popular in the fall, but outdoor signage and a call to their offices will give you the detailed information.

~ 65 ~

Have a Taste of Mexico on Main

That's the name of this authentic Mexican restaurant at 311 North Main. Their extensive menu will amaze you, but my recommendation is to start with a frozen margarita, nibble on their complimentary chips and hot sauce, and then order their fajitas [I love the chicken.] If you visit on a busy day or evening, you'll enjoy "people watching" from their huge front windows.

~ 66 ~

Visit Trains on Main

Trains are very visible on Main Street, from the two cabooses on the railroad track in Frontier Park to the nearby MKT Depot, which has undergone many periods of restoration. It is a perfect place for many special events in our town. If you can visit North Main Street between Thanksgiving and Christmas, you'll see an awesome exhibit of trains in the shop windows, plus an interactive model display. It makes for a very nostalgic experience for the holiday season.

~ 67 ~

Visit a St. Charles Neighborhood House Tour

There are several house tours in the Historic District residential neighborhoods. At Christmas, the Midtown and Commons neighborhoods take turns putting on a tour of six to eight houses that are beautifully decorated for the holidays. Most have been restored, and the clever decorating ideas in these older homes will amaze you. The Midtown neighborhood presents a Garden Tour in the spring that is delightful. I once lived in this storybook area, and I believe the back yards are their castles. The Tourist and Visitors Center on Main Street will give you ticket information. Tickets go quickly for these tours, so call 636-946-7776.

BEAR FACTORY

~ 68 ~

Stuff and Create Your Bear

St. Charles has had a Bear Factory for many years. It is located at 311 S. Main, and even if you don't go in and make a bear, you'll enjoy the fun bear scenes in their large storefront windows. They have 5,000 collectible bears to choose from, and children love special parties in the "Stuffin' Station."

~ 69 ~

Tour a New Town in the Old Town

Duplicating something old in a new community is a very unique and trendy way of development in cities today, and St. Charles is no exception. To the north of town, in what used to be farmland, is a town being built in 1800s-style architecture. It includes homes, business, schools, churches and even entertainment venues such as an amphitheater. To see this amazing reproduction, where people can walk to work, home and entertainment, is worth the visit. Learn more about it on their Web site www.newtownatstcharles.com.

~ 70 ~

Enjoy the Blues

Mark the middle of September to experience a Blues Festival on North Main Street. Pubs and restaurants feature various blues bands after 8:00 p.m. It's fun to visit different locations until you find your favorite. Some are on outdoor patios, since it's a nice time of the year. You'll be singing the blues.

ANGEL OF HOPE

~ 71 ~

Walk Through a Sunken Garden

The Rau Garden is located in the Blanchette Park, at 1900 Randolph Street. Nestled in the 42-acre park is a breathtaking, rectangular garden designed and groomed in beautiful flowers. This garden has a rich history. You will smell the roses and also notice the "Angel of Hope" monument, which was dedicated in 1998 to give peace and hope for those who have lost children. Each December 6th at 7:00 p.m., a candlelight vigil is conducted. Bricks laid around the stone are inscribed with names of children who are no longer with us.

~ 72 ~

Grab a Kart and Go

Grand Prix Karting on Hwy. 94 North can make you feel like a kid again. Weather permitting, March through December, you'll experience Missouri's largest Go Kart track. Karts are available for kids and adults, and picnic grounds and refreshments are available. Hours are 11:00 a.m. to midnight. Call 636-940-7700 for more information.

~ 73 ~

A Place To Reflect or Meditate

As you enter McNair Park at 3200 Droste Road, it would be easy to drive by this secluded area to the right, which was created by our St. Charles Lions club. The club's mission has always been to assist the blind or the sight impaired, so they created a path that you can follow in Braille. For others, the visual is awesome, with a waterfall, beautiful flowers and a pond of water lilies. It is a place to rest, reflect or meditate as you listen to the water fall into the pond. A very special addition to an already beautiful park.

~ 74 ~

Celebrate With the Germans

German Heritage is rich in St. Charles, whose Sister City is Ludwigsburg, Germany. The two cities exchange students and citizens on a regular basis. The Sister Cities Organization helps to produce the annual Oktoberfest, which features a hometown parade. You'll find crafts and German foods in Frontier Park, and the event is topped off with a Burgermeister Ball at Stegton's Banquet Center. German music and dancing are the activities, with German food prepared by German shop owners.

~ 75 ~

Attend the Local Theater

Lindenwood University's Theater is amazingly good and chooses the best for local citizens and students. Jelkyl Theater on the Roemer main campus is where you'll find these up-close and personal productions. I have seen countless shows, but A CHRISTMAS CAROL, shown every holiday season, is always a new surprise. For ticket information, call 636-949-2000.

ABBEY'S VINTAGE SHOP

~ 76 ~

Visit a Real Vintage Clothing Store

You can't walk down North Main Street without stopping at 113 N. Main. The 1940s mannequins in these historic storefront windows are cleverly dressed. Abbey's Vintage Shop displays many periods of vintage clothing and accessories that will take you on a trip to the past. The tastefully displayed inventory sometimes has never been used. You can position yourself in front of the mirror to try on hats and antique jewelry, or decide to rent or buy for your own pleasure. Remember to strike a pose. Call 636-255-0679 for shop hours.

~ 77 ~

Fleur De Lis Market

In the heart of our Historic North Second Street in Frenchtown, you'll discover the feel of Europe as you enjoy this neighborhood event. Besides the interesting shops lined up on the street, you'll be able to enjoy antiques, herbs, flowers and vintage charm. The wine and music add to your enjoyment. This is a one-day-only event on the second Saturday of June. The hours are 10:00 a.m. to 7:00 p.m. Call 636-723-1665 for additional information.

~ 78 ~

See an Indoor Football Game

Based in St. Charles, the River City Rage NIFL Team plays football in the indoor Family Arena. Teams from across the country compete with each other in hard-hitting, "in your face" action. This is for football fans to enjoy all year 'round. Check their Web page, www.ragefootball.com, for scheduled games, or call their office at 636-916-0132.

~ **79** ~

Get Hot, Sauce and Spices Galore

The owner of "Figuero's" at 524 S. Main is "hot" to tell you about the 2100-plus sauces that he markets all over the country. Coffees, teas and accessories fill many rooms that will amaze you! The "Old Town Spice Shoppe" at 334 S. Main will thrill any chef who views and samples the many fresh spices, dips and pastas. "Main Street Market Place" at 708 S. Main is another "hot" spot to taste many delicacies as you shop the country décor merchandise. The street's pretty "hot," don't you think?

~ 80 ~

Attend an Outdoor Church Service

On the Sunday morning during the Lewis and Clark Heritage Days, an ecumenical church service is conducted in Frontier Park at 9:00 a.m. The service is mostly attended by costumed participants of the Heritage Days, but it attracts others like me as well. You feel very close to God by the river's edge. Every year a different pastor conducts the service, which is about 45 minutes long. Song sheets are handed out so you can join in this spiritual tradition.

ST. CHARLES HISTORICAL SOCIETY MUSEUM

~ 81 ~

Check out St. Charles' Heritage

Right in the heart of the downtown area is the St. Charles Historical Society Museum. That means that you can tour the first floor of this onetime City Hall to view the museum's exhibits and then go to the second floor to research your long-lost relatives from St. Charles County. The Curator and many trained volunteers are there to assist you and love doing so. You will also be tempted to purchase one of many available publications on St. Charles. The museum is located at 101 S. Main and open for general research Mondays, Wednesdays and Fridays from 10:00 a.m. to 3:00 p.m.; May through September, it also is open on Saturdays from 10:00 a.m. to 3:00 p.m.

~ 82 ~

We Can Meet You at a Circus

Every year at the end of April, the Moolah Circus comes to our town. We are treated to an outstanding parade in the Historic District on that Saturday, and then you can attend the circus at the Family Arena. You don't have to be a kid to enjoy the fun. You can call the ticket office at 314-534-1111 or get tickets online at www.Metrotix.com.

~ 83 ~

Like to Antique?

St. Charles Antique Mall at #1 Charlestowne Plaza has 30,000 square feet with 250 display booths and 225 show cases. They take pride in their clean, beautiful displays reputable dealers. Call 636-939-4178 for directions if needed. They are open every day! Historic Main Street and our Frenchtown districts also have many privately owned shops to please you as well.

~ 84 ~

Learn to Make Your Own Wine or Beer and Sample the Best

Right in the middle of Second Street in Frenchtown, Frenchtown Cellars will give you a crash course on the secrets of making beer and wine, as well as vinegar and mead. The Cellar has equipment and supplies for helping you to accomplish this unique endeavor. Their hours are Tuesday-Friday 4:45-7:00 p.m., and Saturdays 9:00 a.m. to 3:00 p.m. Call 636-925-9943 if you would like to know more.

~ 85 ~

Experience What a Large Sewing and Quilting Expo Is Like

Every year at the St. Charles Convention Center, you'll be amazed at what fashions are being created and how artistic the quilting industry has become. The expo is conducted by Round Bobbin, whose company organizes events like this in several parts of the country. Celebrities and teachers in the industry are brought in for lectures and classes. You'll see a fashion show and an awesome display of more than 200 quilts. If you haven't seen the latest technology in sewing and quilting, you'll be blown away. Call 1-800-4SEWING for more information, or visit them on the Web at www.roundbobbin.com.

GENERAL STORE

~ 86 ~

Walk into Memory Lane

There's no doubt you will go down memory lane when you walk into the General Store at 322 S. Main. It was established in the late 1970s by "Pop" House, who had a real feel for an old-time general store. He carried tin signs, collectibles, Depression glass, tinware, and, in his most popular counter, penny candy. New owners have carried on "Pop's" tradition since his passing. When you visit, you'll be saying, "Oh, I remember that."

~ 87 ~

Say What, a Boar's Head Festival

A wonderful Christmas tradition takes place every year at Immanuel Lutheran Church, located at 6th and Jefferson. After Thanksgiving, there are two weekends that are dedicated to presenting a Boar's Head Festival right in the main church. More than a hundred actors garbed in elaborate costumes will present songs, dancing and ceremony, celebrating the birth of the Christ Child. This event attracts all Christian denominations. Tickets are hard to come by, so call early. The number is 636-946-2656.

~ 88 ~

Let's Bowl

Generations have been bowling at Plaza Lanes in St. Charles. Located off the Interstate at 506 Droste Road, Plaza Lanes is open every day. If you have children with you, they have kids' bumper bowling. There is always much activity and fun. On the premises is Tubby's Pub 'n Grub, which serves outstanding steaks and hamburgers. What a great combo visit! Call 636-724-1350 for hours.

WORKING POTTER

~ 89 ~

Observe a Working Potter

Located in the oldest Main Street building, where Louis Blanchette settled in 1769, is Plank Road Pottery. This charming, restored building, set back from busy Main Street, is at 906 S. Main. Inside you'll find the finest pottery made in Missouri. Watch as the working potter creates his newest pot, waiting to be fired. You'll find 19th-century art and handmade dulcimers. See them on the Web at www.refinersfirepottery.com or give them a call at 636-255-0530.

~ 90 ~

Hunter and Fisher's Dream

The Bass Pro Shop is more than a unique place to shop, it is an experience, with many exciting outdoor displays to entice any fisherman or hunter. This is the most visited destination in St. Charles. Would you like to see a 6700-gallon aquarium? How about an archery lane and a huge boat showroom? Bass Pro Shop is located right off Interstate 70 near the bridge. The line of cars will take you there.

~ 91 ~

Practice Your Golf Swing

Cave Springs Golf Center is right off the Interstate on the Service Road, at 3650 W. Clay. This long-established center has two grass mats, 15 covered mats, and 20 uncovered mats, and purchases new golf balls every year for your enjoyment. Hours are 9:00 a.m. to 9:00 p.m., and it is well lighted for evening enjoyment. Call 636-723-7272.

THE GLASS WORKBENCH

~ 92 ~

Create Your Own Stained Glass

When you walk into The Glass Workbench at 318 S. Main, you will receive all the attention you need to create your own piece of stained glass, and you even have the option to make a small shade for one of the many lamp bases that they have to offer. You may be happy with a small window ornament, but many options are there for you to experience. Walking amidst all the color sparks your creativity. Handle carefully.

~ 93 ~

*How about a
Walk-in Workout?*

Main Street Gym is used to regulars and visitors walking in
to take advantage of the many services they provide. Located
at 334 North Main, the newly remodeled gym has the latest
equipment and certified staff on hand to provide advice and
assistance. One-on-one Pilates and special assistance for
persons with medical circumstances are an added bonus.
Stop by anytime if you need a quick tan or a chair massage.
Call 636-946-4100 for gym hours or see their Web site at
www.mainstreetgym.com.

~ 94 ~

Attention, Men: Shop at Thro's (Since 1898)

A men's store of this nature and content exists nowhere else in retail today. Thro's Clothing, at 229 North Main Street, is the oldest family-owned business in St. Charles County. It dresses men from their hats to their shoes. Their niche in oversized men's famous-brand clothing is unique in today's market. The Boy Scouts of America Department in the rear of the store has served many generations. Thro's is open every day but Sunday.
Call 636-724-0132 for more information.

FARMER'S MARKET

~ 95 ~

Go to a Farmer's Market

Located in a parking lot on the northern portion of Frontier Park is our own St. Charles Farmer's Market. It's fun to get up early each Saturday morning and get the very best choice of fruits, vegetables, herbs, and even flowers. Local farmers faithfully participate from May to October to bring you high-quality product. It's fun to see the local clientele exchange visits, and maybe go for a cup of coffee together on nearby Main Street.

~ 96 ~

Take Time for a Massage

Salon de Criste is the place to feel good, look good and be seen in St. Charles. This lovely, full-service facility is located at 2880 W. Clay, adjacent to Interstate 70. There's nothing like their basic, therapeutic massage, but there are many body and hair treatments for you to choose from. The ST. CHARLES COUNTY BUSINESS RECORD has ranked this Salon number one in the County. Their national recognition is impressive as well. This is a healthy as well as beautifying experience that you'll love. Visit www.salondecriste.com for details on services or call for an appointment at 636-946-2805.

~ 97 ~

View an Outdoor Friday Night Flick

The fourth Friday night of each month, May through September, you can enjoy the outdoors at Blanchette Landing in the Frenchtown Historic District while you watch a movie. You don't have to bring popcorn because the Neighborhood Association will have refreshments right on the grounds. You'll see "family friendly" movies, so bring the whole gang. Movies start at dark, but for more information, call 636-925-9943.

~ 98 ~

Lewis and Clark Heritage Days

The third full weekend in May is devoted to celebrating the reenactment of Lewis and Clark's encampment in 1804 prior to the exploration of the Louisiana Purchase. This event in the Historic area includes parades of fife-and-drum corps. Witness reenactors, and then visit a military encampment. I enjoy the authentic food in the park, especially the gumbo. You'll be able to share this history we are most proud of.

~ 99 ~

Visit a Cemetery with a Unique Memorial

A heart-wrenching memorial in St. Charles Memorial Gardens marks the site of a deadly accident in 1870. Surrounded by ornate metal fencing is a smokestack and cable that honors the 18 men who were killed when they were hoisting a four-ton column in the construction of the first Wabash Railroad that crossed the Missouri River. There are two signs listing their names. When you turn into the cemetery from West Clay Street, you turn to the right and the memorial is on the corner, hard to miss.

LEWIS, CLARK AND SEAMAN STATUE

~ 100 ~

Visit and Pose with Lewis, Clark and Seaman the Dog

The three are quite a show stopper when you are driving down Riverside Drive, along the river. This 14-foot monument features Meriwether Lewis and William Clark alongside the Newfoundland dog, Seaman. This famous sculpture is by Pat Kennedy of Colorado. Surrounded by beautiful landscaping and with a backdrop of the riverfront park, this is the spot to climb and strike a pose.

ANN HAZELWOOD IN FRONT OF PATCHES, ETC.

Ann Hazelwood loves St. Charles! She has been a resident for 35 years and a St. Charles business owner of Patches etc., for more than 25 years.

She is married to Keith Hazelwood, a local attorney in St. Charles, and has two sons, Joel and Jason, and two sons by marriage, Rocky and Robert.

Giving back to the community has always been important in Ann's life. Her civic activity has included serving as president of organizations such as the Junior Service League, South Main Preservation Society, St. Charles Chamber of Commerce and St. Charles League of Chambers.

Special recognition has not only been given to her within her own quilting industry, as a shop owner and quilt appraiser, but she has received awards in the community, such as "Small Business Person of the Year," "Retailer of the Year" and the "St. Charles Chamber of Commerce's Lifetime Civic Award."

Ann feels that St. Charles offers many unique experiences and wants to share them with YOU!

Other books from

Virginia Publishing

So, Where'd You Go to High School? Vols. 1 & 2

Meet Me in the Lobby: The Story of Harold Koplar
and the Chase Park Plaza

Sweetness Preserved: The Story of Crown Candy Kitchen

Lost Caves of St. Louis

Meeting Louis at the Fair

Still Shining! Discovering Lost Treasures
from the 1904 World's Fair

AND MANY MORE!

www. STL-BOOKS.com